©2021 - All rights reserved.

The content contained within this book may not be reproduced, duplicated, or transmitted without direct written permission from the publisher.

Under no circumstances will any blame or legal responsibility be held against the publisher, or author, for any damages, reparation, or monetary loss due to the information contained within this book, either directly or indirectly.

Legal Notice:
This book is copyright protected. It is only for personal use. You cannot amend, distribute, sell, use, copy or edit any part, or the content within this book, without the consent of the publisher.

By reading this document, the reader agrees that under no circumstances is the author responsible for any losses, direct or indirect, that are incurred as a result of the use of the information contained within this document, including, but not limited to, errors, omissions, or inaccuracies.

SPECIAL BONUS!

for houseplant lovers.

Make caring for your houseplants easier with this logbook.

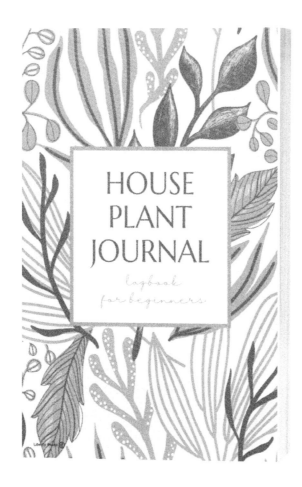

Get the ready-to-print logbook for FREE,
Plus, all my new books by joining the fan base!

SCAN WITH YOUR MOBILE PHONE **TO JOIN!**

Pothos

💧 Can be grown in dry soil or a vase of water

☀ Does well in bright, indirect light as well as low light

Snake Plants

 Let them dry out between watering

 Likes bright indirect sunlight

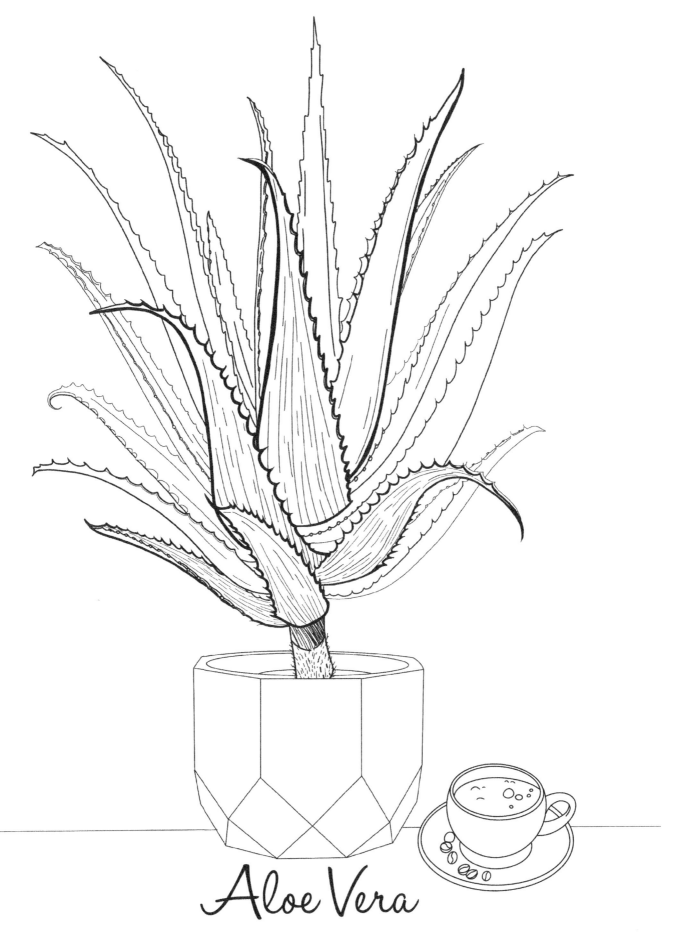

Aloe Vera

 Let them dry out between watering ☼ Likes bright indirect sunlight

Haworthia

 Water every 2-3 weeks

 Can be in direct sunlight and tolerate medium light

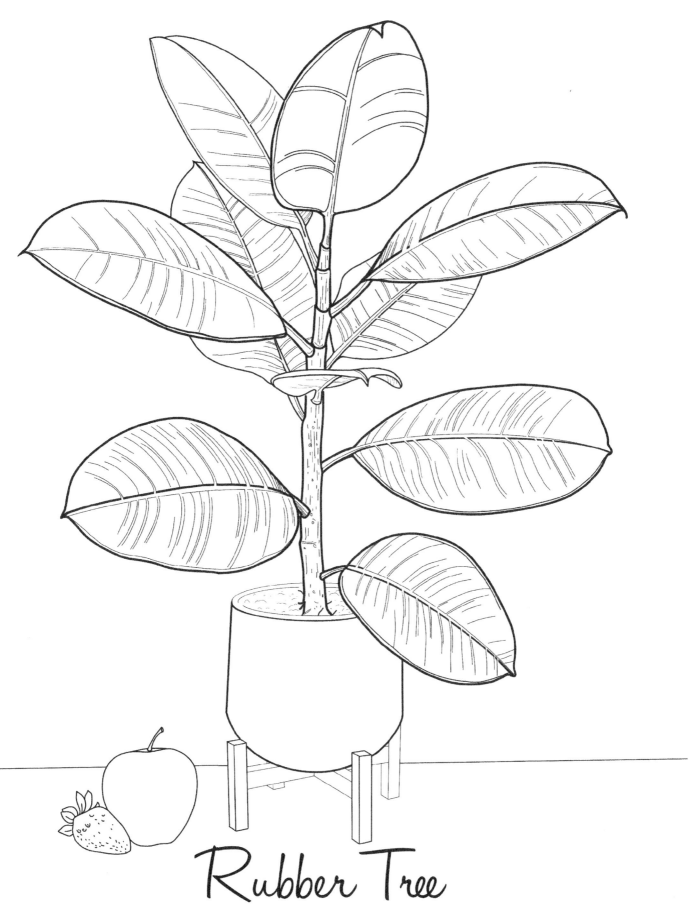

Rubber Tree

 Water every other day   65 - 85 F   Mist during any season if they air is too dry

Calathea Roseopicta "Dottie"

 Keep the soil moist but not soak

 Likes warm temperature

Scan to see plant ref

Calathea Ornata

 Keep the soil moist but not soak

 Place in bright iindirect sunlight

 Scan to see plant ref

Stromanthe sanguinea "Triostar"

 Keep the soil moist but not soak

☼ Bright iindirect sunlight. Burns easily in sunlight.

 Scan to see plant ref

Calathea Warscewiczii

 Likes consistent soil moisture

 Bright iindirect sunlight and warm temperatures

 Scan to see plant ref

Calathea Zebrina

 65-85℉ Intolerant to colder temperatures

 Likes moist but well drained soil

 Scan to see plant ref

Calathea Lancifolia

 Bright indirect sunlight and warm temperatures

 Keep moist. Never allow it to dry out

 Scan to see plant ref

Calathea Roseopicta "Rosey"

 Very sensitive, keep away from strong direct sunlight

 Water thoroughly once the top inch of soil feels dry

 Scan to see plant ref

Calathea Burle Marxii

 Keep soil lightly moist

 Slightly poisonous, keep away from children and pets

 Scan to see plant ref

Hoya Burtoniae

 Wilts or droops when it's time for water.

 Fertilize once a month is sufficient

 Scan to see plant ref

Hoya Rubra Krimson Princess

 Likes chunky, light and airy soil

☼ Variegated plants need more indirect sunlight as the variegation does not help the plant to photosynthesize.

 Scan to see plant ref

Hoya Carnosa Variegata

 Allow water to drain out completely before watering

 Do not place in a bright window with unfiltered light, the leaves will bleach yellow and fall off

 Scan to see plant ref

Hoya Pubicalyx

 Drought-tolerant houseplant but water regularly in the growing season.

 Use a light, airy, and well-drained soil mixture

 Scan to see plant ref

Hoya Obovata

💧 Wait until the soil has dried out, then water thoroughly

☀ Full sun-bright, indirect light

 Scan to see plant ref

Hoya Memoria (Gracilis)

 Loves Lightweight, fast-draining potting mix

 Likes to be root bound. Need to be repotted very seldom

Hoya Macrophylla

 Rainwater or distilled water for watering. Avoid using tap water at all times.

Cannot tolerate direct sunlight exposure too much

 Scan to see plant ref

Hoya Caudata

 Loves more than 60% humidity

Prefers 65-95°F Intolerant to colder temperatures and in-direct sunlight

Hoya Retusa

 If the leaves becoming crisp and brown, this is a sign that the humidity may be lacking.

 Fertilize only once a month

Hoya Linearis

💧 Likes to dry out well between watering.

💧 Water until all the soil is saturated and all excess water drains away through the drainage hole

Hoya Carnosa

  Loves high humdity

  Easily propagated by cuttings

Philodendron 'Brasil'

 Allow the topsoil to dry out waterings

 Loves bright indirect sunlight

Philodendron Xanadu

☼ Needs more light than other Philo

💧 Allow top 50% of the soil to dry out before watering

"Silver leaf Philodendron"

 Allow upper layer to dry out before watering

 Above-average humidity levels. increase humidity by misting

Heartleaf Philodendron

 Loves a good soaking and then allow the top half of the soil to dry out before watering again.

All Philodendron plants are poisonous

Philodendron Micans

Looks a lot like the typical heart-leaf philodendron but with beautiful velvet finish.

 Watering when the top inch or so of soil dries out

Philodendron Hastatum

 Give it a big splash once a week

Philodendron 'White Wizard'

 Keep the soil moist at all times but avoid excessive water

☼ Loves mild filtered sunlight

 Scan to see plant ref

Philodendron Mexicanum

 Enjoys moist but not wet soil   Loves 70%-85% filtered sunlight

Philodendron 'Pink Princess'

 Do not put it in direct light, or its beautiful leaves may scorch.

 Scan to see plant ref

Philodendron 'Paraiso Verde'

 The variegations will turn dark green if the plant receives too much light.

 Scan to see plant ref

Philodendron Birkin

 Thrive from bright indirect light

 Grows the best in sphagnum peat moss-based soil

Philodendron Melanochrysum

 Prefers bright shade, filtered sunlight or indirect bright light

 Needs well-draining soil but keep moist

Monstera

 Water your Monstera when the top 50-75% of the soil is dry

 Can grow just about anywhere in your home! It tolerates low light, but grows faster and becomes more dramatic under indirect bright light.

Alocasia 'Silver Dragon'

 Place in bright dappled sunlight

 Use well draining airy soil with calcium rich fertilizer

 Scan to see plant ref

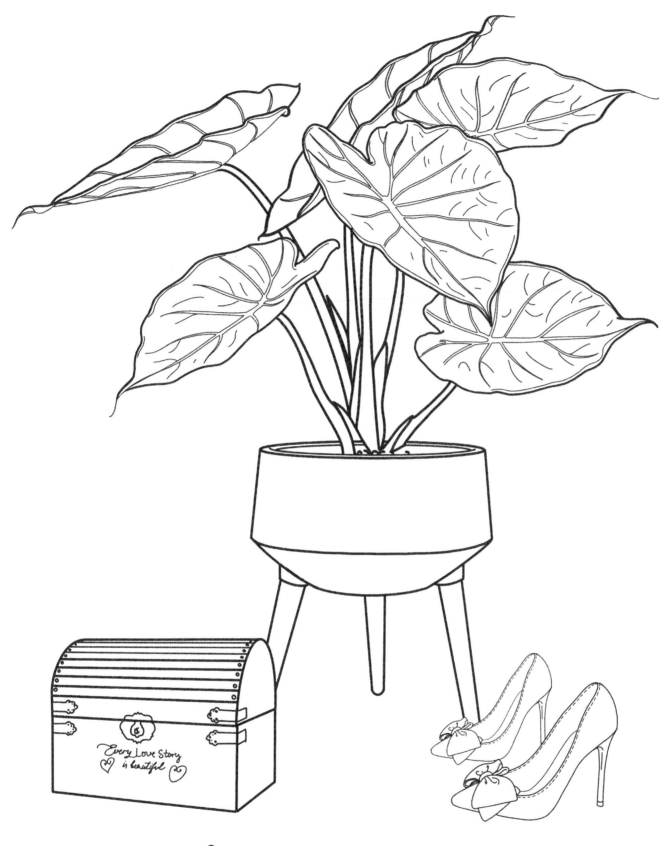

Alocasia wentii

 Prefers bright indirect light, but tolerates direct sunlight in the late afternoon or early morning.

 Maintain lightly moist conditions. Very prone to root rot if overwatered, but cannot tolerate dry soil..

Alocasia cuprea 'Red Secret'

 Allow to fully dry between watering

 Soggy soil and wet leaves can lead to fungal infectioins

 Scan to see plant ref

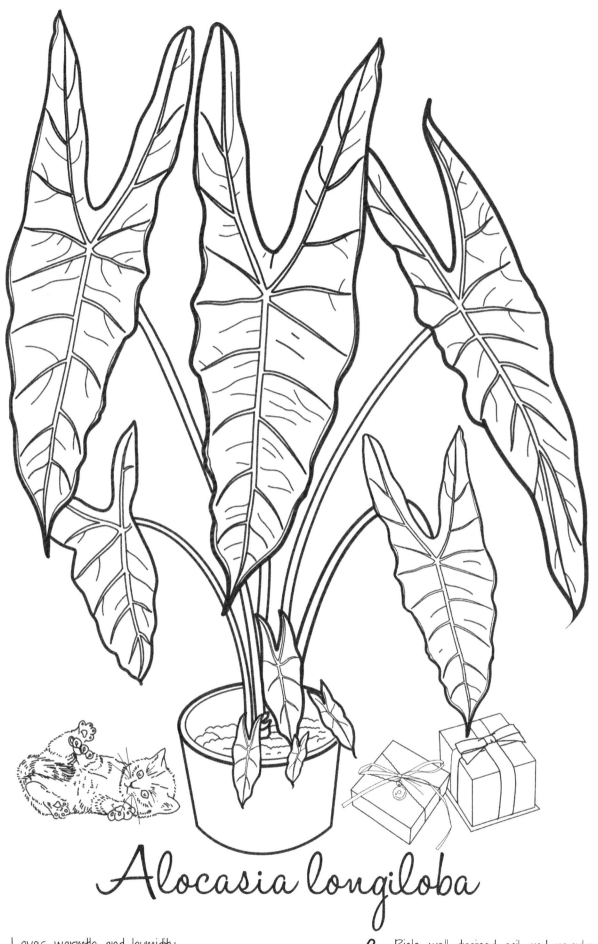

Alocasia longiloba

 Loves warmth and humidity.
Dry air can lead to diseases i.e. red spider mites

 Rich, well drained soil and regular watering, especially when larger

Alocasia reginula 'Black Velvet'

 Allow the top two inches of soil to dry before watering.

 Feed monthly with a balanced fertilizer.

 Scan to see plant ref

Alocasia 'Dragon Scale'

 Bright, indirect light. Direct sunlight will scorch the leaves

 Never fertilise in winter

 Scan to see plant ref

Green Velvet Alocasia

 Bright, indirect light. Avoid more than 1-2 hours of direct sunlight.

 Alocasia Frydek benefits from regular fertilizer while actively growing

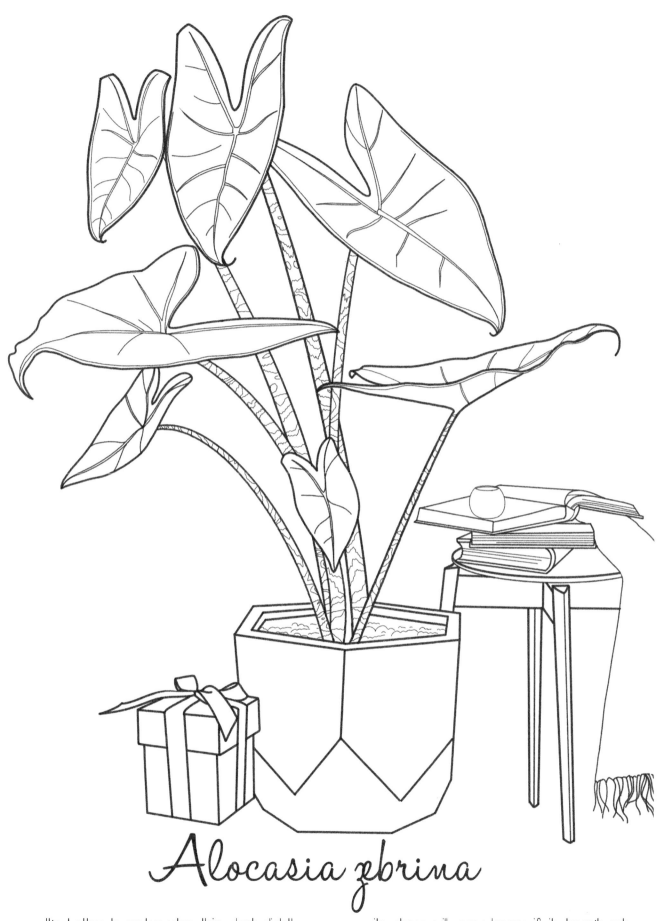

Alocasia zebrina

 It's better to underwater this plant slightly because Its thick stems contain a lot of moisture

 Its stems will grow longer if it doesn't get enough light. Keep rotating after water if it does.

Alocasia Amazonica 'Polly'

 Appreciates being placed in a humid environment

 Keep away from small children and pets

 Scan to see plant ref

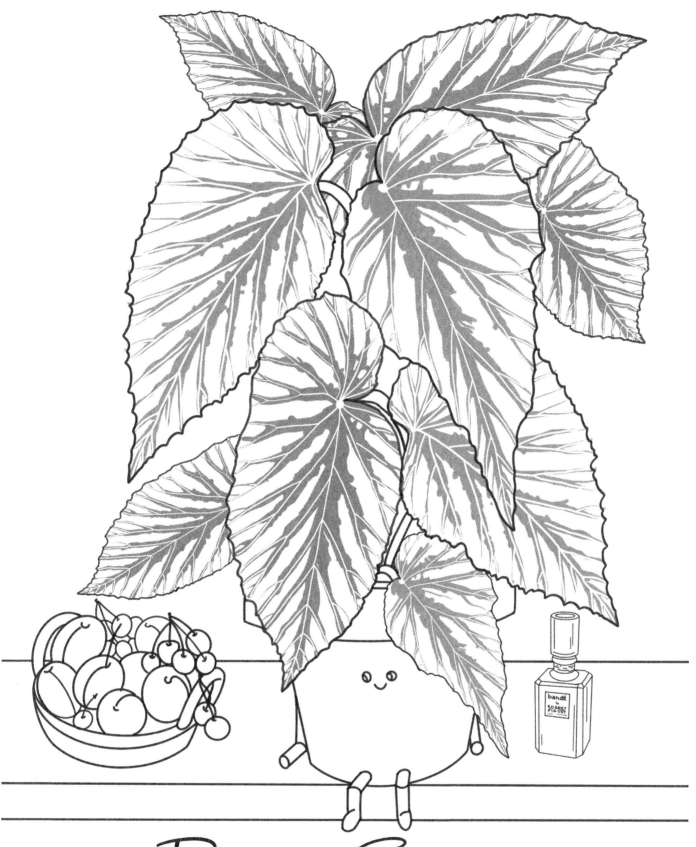

Begonia Exotica

 Avoid direct sun as it will burn the leaves

Scan to see plant ref

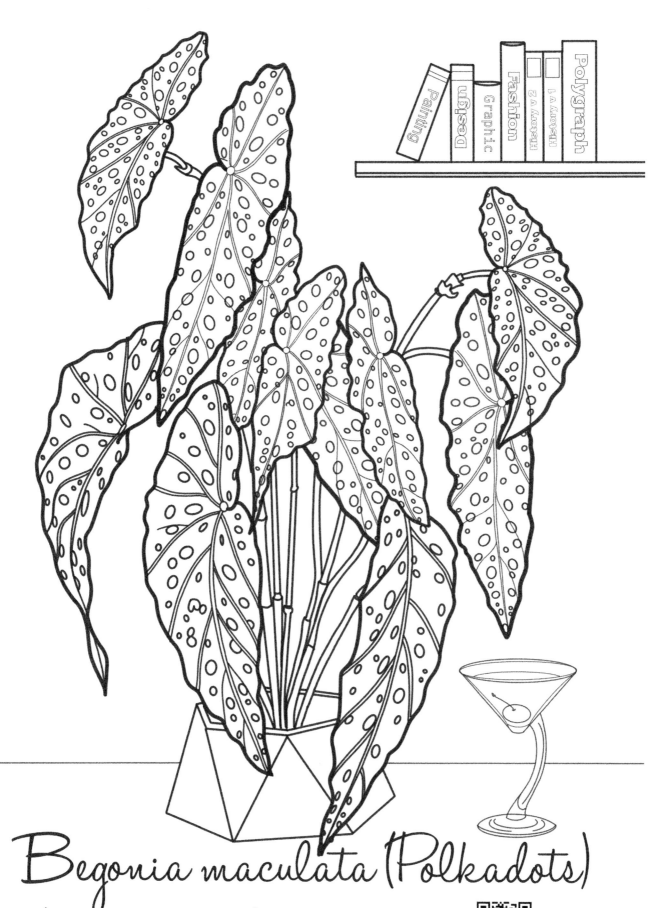

Begonia maculata (Polkadots)

 Let the soil dry a bit before watering

☀ Leaves can burn with too much sun

 Scan to see plant ref

Begonia 'Angel Wing'

 Can't handle direct sunlight

 Moist soil mixture but not soggy, includes a lot of organic matter

 Scan to see plant ref

Fairy Rex Begonia

 High levels of humidity, 50% or above

 Prefers a moist but well draining soil and a slightly acidic or neutral compost mix.

 Scan to see plant ref

Duarten Rex Begonia

 ILkes bright, indirect light year-round

 Airy, light, fast-draining soil is best

 Scan to see plant ref

Ballet Rex Begonia

 Use distilled water because tap water has high mineral salt content, causing leaf edge burn.

 Scan to see plant ref

Tornado Rex Begonia

 High levels of humidity, 50% or above

 Scan to see plant ref

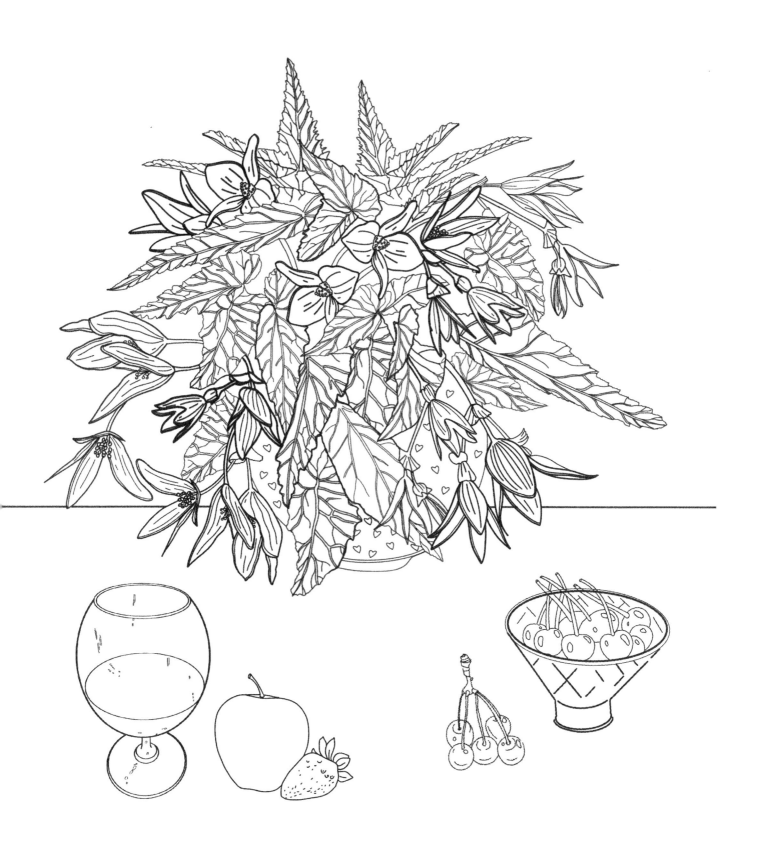

Begonia 'Waterfall'

 Likes well-drained clay, loamy, sandy soil

 Scan to see plant ref

Begonia 'Glowing Embers'

 Morning light or light that is filtered through leaves or a lattice roof helps with flowering

 Scan to see plant ref

Anthurium Clarinervium

 After you water thoroughly, make sure you discard excess water.

☀ Keep these plants away from too much direct sun.

 Scan to see plant ref

Anthurium Veitchii

 Humidity high above 60%

 A light aroid potting mix using perlite, orchid bark, and peat moss

Anthurium warocqueanum

 Humidity high above 70%

watering frequent but light. Try to keep the soil moist

 Scan to see plant ref

Scherzer's Anthurium

 Water your plant regularly, but make sure that the water drains out of the pot quickly

Any loose, well drained soil will work wel

 Scan to see plant ref

Anthurium Forgetii

 Likes a good dose of bright indirect sunlight throughout the day

 soil should remain slightly moist throughout the growing season

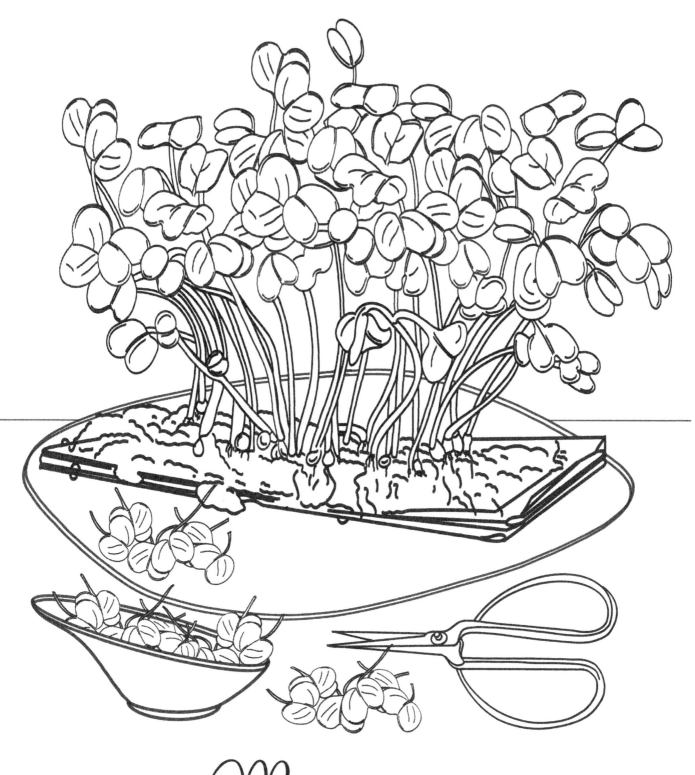

Micro green

💧 Keep an eye on the colour of the soil. If it is a glossy black it has enough water. If it is more of a dull black, then it needs water

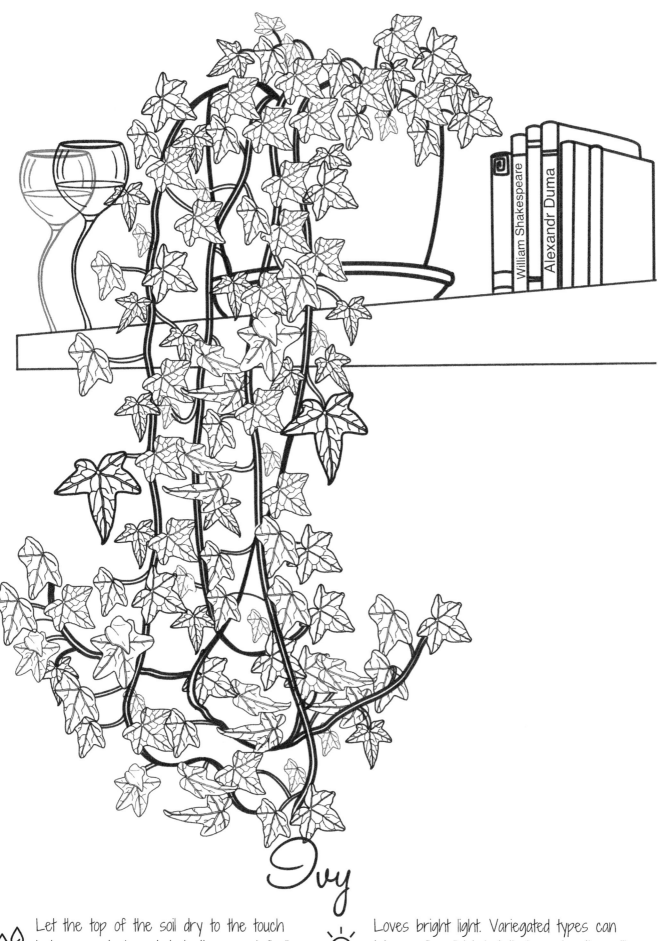

Ivy

💧 Let the top of the soil dry to the touch between waterings. Wash them periodically to remove dust and pests from the leaves.

☀ Loves bright light. Variegated types can take medium light, but their variegation will become less pronounced in less light

Peperomia caperata

💧 Allow the soil to dry out slightly between waterings

☀ Low to bright light. Light from an east- or north-facing window works best

 Scan to see plant ref

Oxalis triangularis

 Water when the top inch of soil becomes dry

☼ Grow in rich, well-drained potting mix

 Scan to see plant ref

Tradescantia 'Tricolor'

 Bright, indirect sunlight. Too little sunlight will result in little variegation. The excessive direct sun causes leaf scorch.

 Too much fertilizer causes leaves to lose variegation.

 Scan to see plant ref

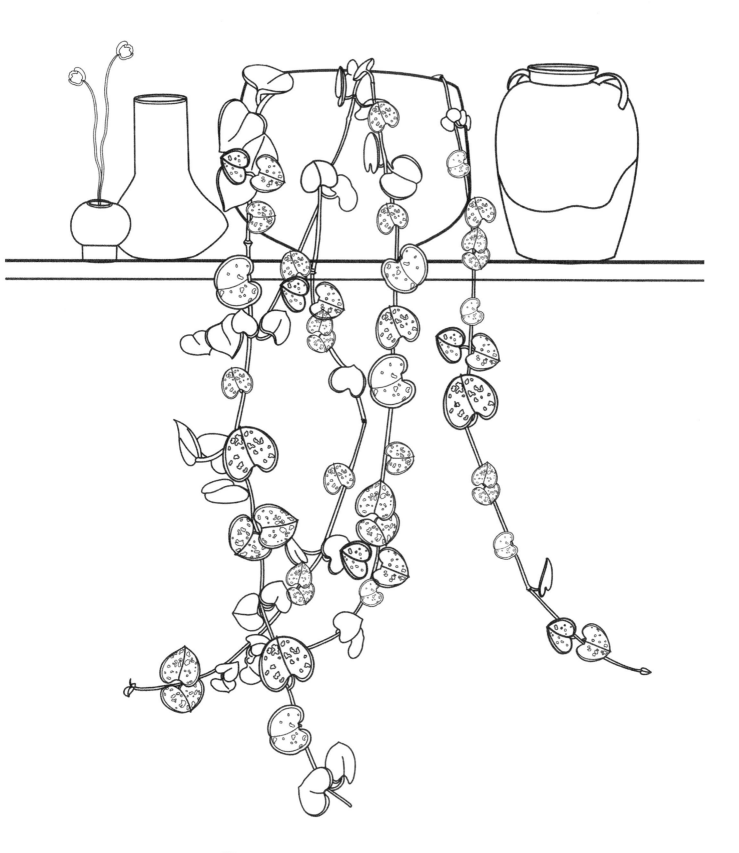

String of hearts

 Bright light, with some direct sun (but not all day))

 whenever the top 2 to 3 inches of the soil is completely dry

 Scan to see plant ref

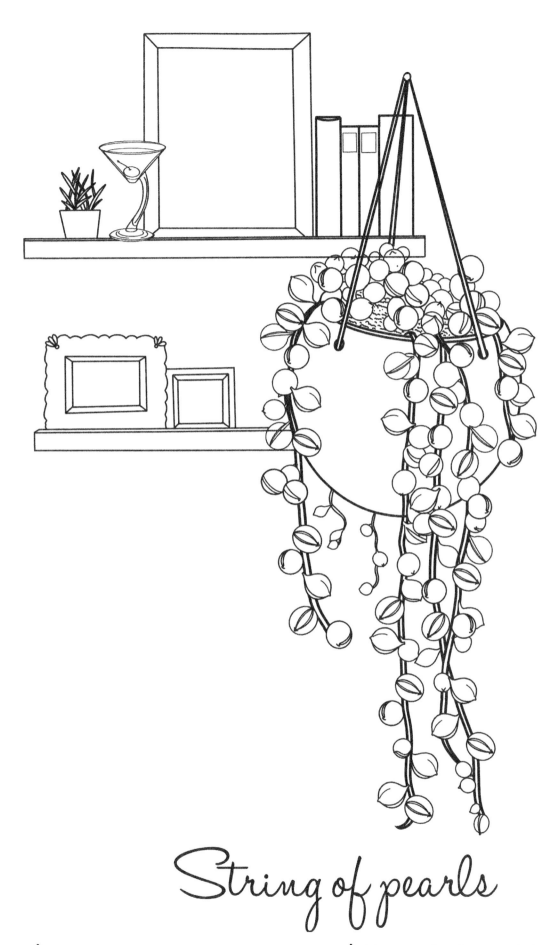

String of pearls

 Only about 40% relative humidity

Very sensitive to overwatering, so make sure that you give them just enough water.

Hippeastrum

 Thrives in full sun or light shade. Ideal planting times Sep - Dec

 Use well-drain soil and water once a week even in dry spells

Bromeliad

 Keep the soil moist, but not soggy

 Requires bright, indirect, sunny spaces

Cereus peruvianus

 Can tolerate medium light or even full sun outdoors

💧 Water once a month. Pour water slowly all around the center of the plant so that it filters down the base

Bird of Paradise

 Allow to dry out slightly between waterings. Enjoy moist but not soggy soil.

Needs bright light, including some direct sunlight, to bloom well

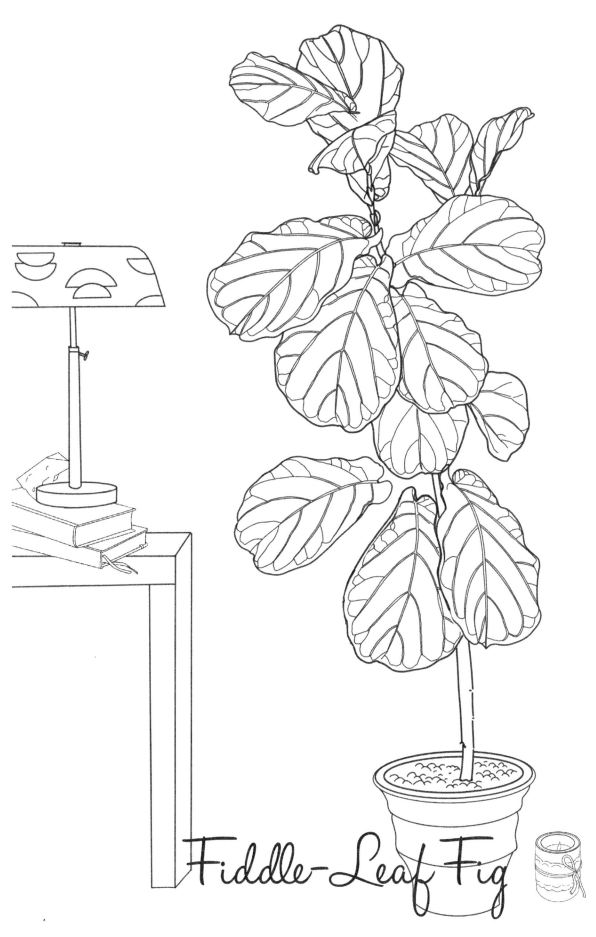

Fiddle-Leaf Fig

 Prefer to dry out slightly between waterings

 need a lot of natural light and do best when placed directly in front of a window

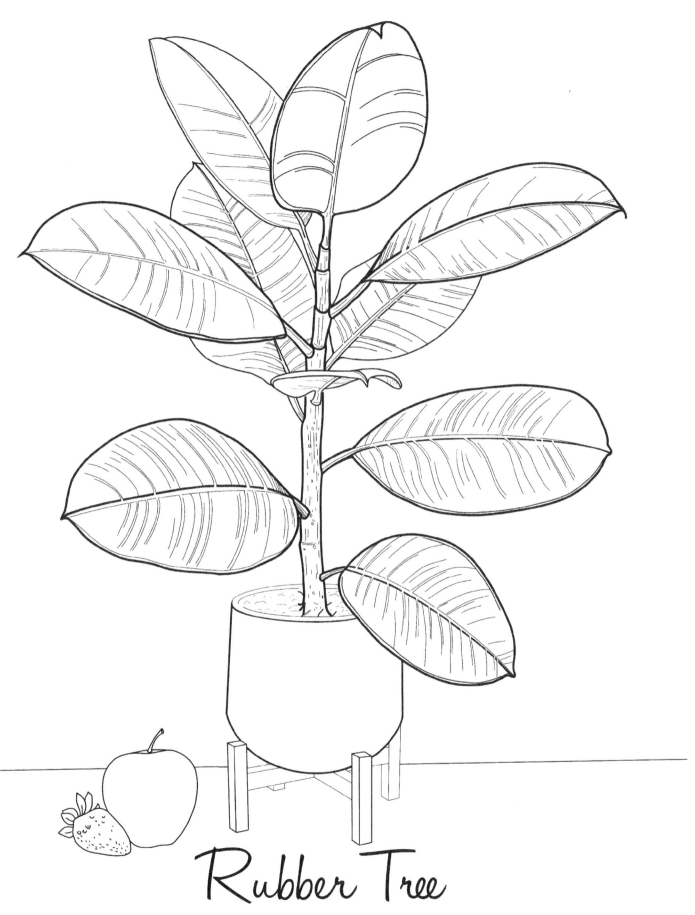

Rubber Tree

💧 Allow soil to dry out between watering.

☀ Thrives in medium to bright indirect light, and can tolerate bright direct light.

Hibiscus chinese

☀ Full sun exposure

 Fertile, loam sandy and loam soils are best

 Scan to see plant ref

SPECIAL BONUS!

for houseplant lovers.

Make caring for your houseplants easier with this logbook.

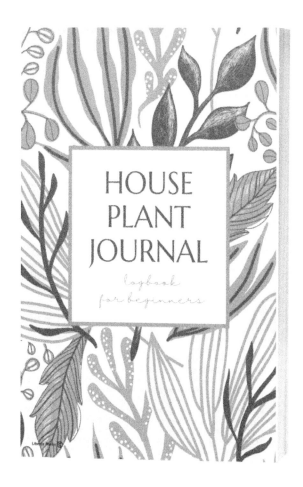

Get the ready-to-print logbook for FREE,
Plus, all my new books by joining the fan base!

SCAN WITH YOUR MOBILE PHONE TO JOIN!

Printed in Great Britain
by Amazon